Honey Suckle Kisses: Poetic Imaginations

By Synthia SAINT JAMES

Copyright 2016 Synthia SAINT JAMES

All rights reserved. No part of this book may be reproduced in any form or by any means without the prior written permission of Synthia SAINT JAMES, excepting brief quotes used in conjunction with reviews, written specifically for inclusion in a magazine or newspaper.

ISBN-13: 978-0692712320
ISBN-10: 0692712321

Author's Preface

The muses have embraced me again.
I began writing poetry in 1970, but this
NEW petite book was written and completed
in May, 2016. AMAZING!!!

I promise that there's more to come.
Hope you ENJOY!!!

In GOLDEN light & love

synthia

Dedicated to my Mom: Hattie
Thank you for GIFTING me with your
love and encouragement in ALL that
I do.

Cover Art: "Erzulie: Haitian Goddess of Love"
Oil and Acrylic on Canvas - 30x24"
Copyright 2012 Synthia SAINT JAMES

Fine Art Reproductions Available
www.synthiasaintjames.com/gallery.html

Wikipedia: en.m.wikipedia.org/wiki/Erzulie

Erzulie Fréda Dahomey, the Rada aspect of Erzulie, is the Haitian African spirit of love, beauty, jewelry, dancing, luxury, and flowers. She wears three wedding rings, one for each husband - Damballa, Agwe and Ogoun. Her symbol is a heart, her colours are pink, blue, white and gold, and her favourite sacrifices include jewellery, perfume, sweet cakes and liqueurs.

You were so stunningly radiant

magically majestic

yet so very real

when I first laid eyes on you

The soft light in the dimly lit room

highlighted and tenderly

embraced your face

like in an exquisite oil painting

from another period

time and place

The essence of the Renaissance

mixed with a touch

of the French Impressionist

Gently outlining

your silky tresses

chiseled features

then, so very seductively

your beautiful expressive eyes

before reaching your sensuous

and slightly pouted lips

I was spellbound

you mesmerized me

and I felt intoxicated

as I continuously stole

secret glances of you

throughout that night

Our eyes almost met

on a few occasions

and when they finally did

you gifted me with

your luminous smile

I was titillated

and must have blushed

wondering if you

had been feeling me

all along

Were you feeling me

all along

The room

was filled with

too many people

so I shyly looked away

My heart was pounding

so very loudly

and my temperature

was certainly rising

as I fumbled

with my purse

Just moments later

when I finally

looked up

you were there

seated right beside me

smiling

You very gently

captured

my hands

in yours

and with introductions made

we began

our first conversation

It must have lasted

for at least an hour

feeling like just minutes

our connection was made

That night when

I finally fell asleep

I had dreams of

honey suckle kisses

tender and sweet embraces

wee mornings, afternoons,

evenings and nights

filled with ecstasy

I had already

fast forwarded

with anticipation

We met for

Sunday brunch

the very next day

Greenwich Village

in a small French café

delicious in so

many ways

Nightly conversations

strolls through

Washington Square

and Central Park

catching The Wiz

on Broadway

Shrimp Scampi

and other delights

at Joe Allen's

the rhythms of jazz

uptown in Harlem

at Smalls Paradise

We prepared

our dinner together

for the first time

You were my

Sous chef

cutting, slicing

chopping and dicing

while we sipped

Beaujolais Nouveau

and listened to the

musical modulations of

Minnie Riperton, Al Jarreau,

and Earth Wind and Fire

Sautéed seasoned scallops

with mushrooms, scallions

and chopped black olives

served over

warm baby spinach

sprinkled with my homemade

French garlic vinaigrette

Sherry baked chicken

and petite baby potatoes

grilled in extra

virgin olive oil

with garlic

a slightly toasted

French baguette

saturated with President Butter

Over my intimately

small dinner table

we lit candles

and offered up grace

to the creator

I watched you

and your bright

sparkling eyes

as we devoured

our meal together

smiling and speaking

between mouthfuls

and enjoying

every single second

After washing

the dishes

we relaxed

on my couch

topping off

then drinking

our unfinished

glasses of wine

our bodies

and minds

took over

A magnificent sky

filled with a kaleidoscope

of brilliant colors

all cadmium in hue

golden yellows and oranges

reds of crimson

and shades of blue

greeted us through

my half-closed blinds

on our first

morning after

as we kissed

and snuggled

even more closely

and slept the rest

of the morning

With stomachs growling

we awoke

famished

fixed our first

break-fast together

leftovers from

the night before

hastily reheated

in my microwave

and quenching our thirst

with chilled glasses

of Sauvignon Blanc

garnished with

thin slices of fresh

ruby red strawberries

showering together

in warm, refreshing

and enticing

jet streams of water

hitting our bodies

in all the right places

taking turns

bathing each other

with lightly scented

peppermint soap

using sponges

and loofahs

while passionately

kissing, touching

and feeling ALL again

from the night before

The universe paused

in wonder and adoration

while the dolphins

playfully leaped

from oceans

and seashores

skylarks and nightingales

expressed their glee

in melodious harmony

all in celebration of

our new found love

Honey suckle kisses

tender and sweet embraces

wee mornings, afternoons,

evenings and nights

filled with ecstasy…

I fell into a deep

hypnotic sleep

aroused by your

fragrant scent

still lingering

so very strongly

on my pillows

and sheets

Dreams of faraway

exotic places

Fiji, Tahiti

the Marquesas

our moist bodies melting

into white sandy beaches

then rejuvenating

in the translucent

aquamarine seas

places we are

destined to visit

I awakened exuberant

and refreshed

feeling adored

exquisite and beautiful

and wrapped

in your love

www.ingramcontent.com/pod-product-compliance
Lightning Source LLC
Chambersburg PA
CBHW060622070426